MW00788614

A Simple Guide to

Creating A
Family History Book

that is interesting, engaging and treasured

by

Marian Rees

Printed in the United Kingdom
A CIP record of this book is available from the British Library

First Printing 2019

ISBN 978-0-9542907-4-0

Chalk Ridge Publications

Dedication

This book is dedicated to my wonderful, ever-patient husband Bill, whose enthusiasm and support throughout our many treks around the country (sunshine and rain!) on the ancestral trail, has been ceaseless.

Contents

Foreword

Family history research can be extremely rewarding, taking the researcher through an entire spectrum of emotions: joy, when an elusive ancestor is named; pride, for those who are found to have done something selfless and brave; excitement, when there is a link to royalty; and sadness, on uncovering the deaths of so many infants and the obvious grief of their parents. There are also the discoveries of legal battles, legacies, successes and hardships.

The journey results in a wealth of information, paperwork and old photographs. But what next? How can we share our research with other family members and pass that knowledge on to future generations?

This book is written in the hope that it might help fellow family historians to commit their family story to print. I do not pretend to be a skilled writer or computer expert, just an amateur with abundant enthusiasm. When I compiled our own family story in 'Apple Pies and Welsh Cakes', I tackled presentation issues and family sequencing problems that had stalled my progress for some considerable time. The overarching obstacle though, was probably the thought that the research was not yet complete. The reality is of course that the research will never be complete – so there is no time like the present!

Good luck!

Marian

Creating an interesting book

I decided at the outset that I wanted our family history to be as informative and readable as possible. This meant trying to shed some light on the lives and characters of our ancestors, not just giving a list of births, deaths and marriages. To this end, the decision was made not to treat the book as an academic exercise with numerous citations and 'footers' filled with document reference numbers. The choice is of course for the individual compiler with regard to the potential audience.

Before starting, gather as much information from relatives: anecdotes, photographs and inherited artefacts are what brings our ancestors to life. If you plan talking to relatives to find out what they remember, a recording device is a great help. It is important though, to tell family members that you are turning the voice recorder on and to check they have no objection. In my experience, the initial reserved silences were quickly overtaken by the enthusiasm for the subject matter. If you are lucky, as I was, elderly relatives living too far for a brief visit may be happy to write down some of their memories. When it comes to the more recent generations you may well have your own experiences to draw on.

A file for each family line, chronologically arranged, is a great help when it comes to writing up your findings. It will help to keep you on track and prevent you from missing out any of your gathered information.

Old photos

The permanent surrender of old photographs will no doubt deter others from searching through their old albums. This can be easily resolved by offering reassurance that the ancient pictures will be photographed (which can be done on the spot) or borrowed, scanned and returned immediately. I found that enhancing my relatively low-cost digital camera with the addition of a zoom lens gave slightly better reproductions.

Relatives living some considerable distance away took their precious photos to be scanned. The images, although not quite as clear as the original photographs were perfectly acceptable for illustration purposes. A few 'tweeks' made them just a little clearer.

Above: The photocopied image of Great Aunt Irene was initially quite pale but using my laptop's pre-installed photo-editing software the image became more defined and could be used successfully in the book.

Some old photos have creases and other areas of damage. This can be expected, especially with regard to photos that have not been kept in albums. Leaving your copy unaltered can add authenticity to your work but in some cases the blemishes detract from the picture and it is possible to 'restore' copies using some simple techniques. Your own computer or laptop will probably have a photographic package as part of the setup. If you are one of the technically advanced you can of course use one of the more complex photo-editing software packages available. But if, like me, you are a novice in these realms, the simpler the better!

Make sure you save your original copy, then use a duplicate copy for experimentation. If you are planning to produce a black and white only book (most old photos are either black and white or sepia coloured) then the first thing to do is to make your image black and white. Contrast or 'clarity' as it is sometimes labelled, is then a good starting point. Photos that have faded can look almost white but when you add contrast the computer image can suddenly come to life. This is also the solution I found best for enhancing photocopies (as illustrated earlier).

These are some of the images that I played with using my Microsoft Photos photo-editing package which came with Windows10:

The crease damage has just been 'coloured in'.

The repair can still be seen but does not detract from the image in the same way.

'Clarity', is the only change here:

Photos will bring your ancestors to life. Sadly, the earliest photos were only usually taken of those who could afford the relatively high fee, when photography was in its infancy.

You may also come across photo images on glass, usually set into gold coloured frames:

You will not want to damage these relatively rare finds but with care it is still possible to photograph the image and include it in your book.

If you are really lucky, in the days pre-dating photographs, you may even find an artist portrait:

This water colour behind glass still has the original framer's details on the reverse. Along with the style of dress, it was possible to date the portrait to around 1820.

Organising Your Book

Sequential Issues

The problems with sequencing family members when putting together the family history in book form rather than as a computer package are surely the most difficult to overcome. Computer packages allow users to hop between family members with no sequencing problems. However, when writing, if you start with the youngest and move to their parents and grandparents, each generation is twice the size of the previous one. It soon becomes unwieldy. In reverse, starting with the earliest ancestor, the same issues present.

With my own book, as my intention was to present the family history of our children, both my family and my husband's family were central. I had been able trace all lines back to our Great Grandparents, many quite a bit further. So that was my starting point. Our sixteen Great Grandparents named the chapters of the book and each named family was taken from the earliest known relative. There was some obvious crossover with the more recent generations but I have to say I was pleased with the result. Named chapters also have the advantage of signposting relatives to the parts of the book that hold the most interest for them.

When writing the book, I found this structure enormously helpful in keeping me on track and my focus on only one part of the family tree at a time. It also gives a clear pathway making it possible to see just how much has been completed and how many family branches are still to be covered at any time.

If you are concentrating on only one family name, researching back through the male line, your sequential issues will be significantly reduced. Beginning with the earliest generation and working through to the present day will give the book a clear pathway.

I made the decision not to focus on the current generation in order to preserve privacy (that will be a task for future generations!).

At the beginning of the book it is a good idea to have a family tree linking the surnames: not everyone will be aware of the surnames of their early ancestors.

The chapters can then start with the detailed part of the family tree relevant to the surname of focus. In the case of a 'one-name' study the detailed part of the tree can relate to the generation of focus. I used a computer package called 'GenoPro' for this (more details are in Chapter 7) but many packages are available and being developed all the time.

Over the course of your family research you will no doubt create a family tree encompassing the whole family with all names and dates (many software packages can achieve this). It is a really good way of seeing how the different family members relate to each other. The whole tree is likely to be vast, making it impossible to include in the pages of a book. Mine, when printed (on numerous A4 sheets of thin card) measures 5 metres long and half a metre high (in approximately font size 11). The solution is to include the full tree on a CD instead (more details in Chapter 11).

A Key to the Family Surnames

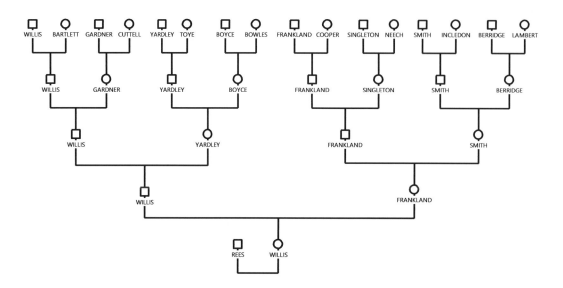

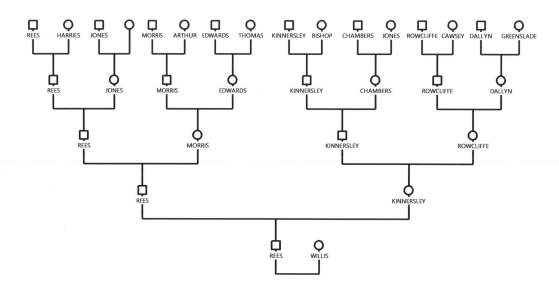

Above is the 'key' to my family and that of my husband. Its purpose is just to act as a signpost for those who are unfamiliar with the family lines.

Formal Records and Other Recorded Evidence

Before starting your family history book, it is necessary to acquire as much information as possible. A great deal can be searched for on-line (the free and subscription sites that I used are detailed in Chapter 6).

Birth, Death and Marriage Certificates

Birth certificates are a must. They started in 1837. From the birth certificate the date of birth, full names of the child, father and mother (including the mother's maiden name) and the occupation of the father are identified, as well as their address at the time of the birth. The name and address of the informant is also given. The informant is usually the mother or father but I was lucky on a few occasions that it was the child's grandmother, so her name and address were suddenly also available to me. Another of the birth certificates that I acquired told me that the child was illegitimate in that no father's name was given. Again, lucky for me the child's middle name was the surname of the natural father (verified through other investigation).

Marriage certificates are also invaluable. Again, they were mandatory from 1837. The marriage certificate gives the date of the marriage, the full names and ages of the bride and groom (although occasionally 'full age' replaces their actual ages), their 'condition' at the time of the marriage (spinster, bachelor, widow or widower) where they were living at the time of their marriage and the occupation of the groom. It also provides the names of the fathers of bride and groom and their occupations. On occasion, one or both fathers may have died prior to the marriage. If this is the case, the names are still given followed by the word 'deceased'. If retired, that is also recorded as well as the job they retired from. Other information is provided about the marriage venue and presiding registrar and those who witnessed the marriage (often other members of the family). The details should all be absolutely trustworthy but a word of warning here: we have one ancestor who, it appears, made a habit of pretending to be younger than his actual age and another who gave her natural father's surname as her maiden name despite contradicting her birth certificate details! It is sometimes these discrepancies that provide pathways to the most intriguing family stories.

Death certificates can be very informative, especially where a younger life is lost. Due to the inherent cost, I limited my purchase of certificates to those who had died post infancy but earlier than the commonplace 50-60 years. The death certificate gives light to much sadder information but finding a death from Cholera where the living conditions were known to be poor, or infectious illness causing the death of a number of siblings while living at close quarters in a workhouse does paint a picture that should be shared. The death certificate gives the date of death and registration; the cause of death and where it happened; and the informant's name and address. It also records the occupation of the deceased person.

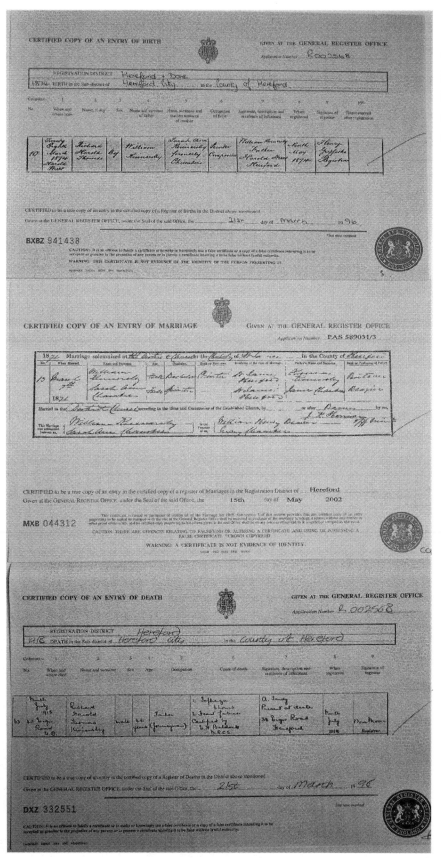

An example of Birth (red), Marriage (green) and Death (black) certificates provided as copies.

Certificates can be ordered from the General Register Office - https://www.gro.gov.uk
(at the time of writing, the cost is £11 per copy or £7 for a PDF to print yourself).

The Census

Census information is really useful and gives a once a decade view of each family group. Following moves of house, changes of occupation and expansion of the family is so important if a story is to be told as accurately as possible. Additionally, look at the neighbouring households. I have often found other family members living very close by, indeed some right next door. It is also possible to find that all households are occupied by workers in a particular industry.

The Census started to be taken in 1831, although very few areas completed or retained this data. The first comprehensive Census was recorded in 1841. This was fairly rudimentary and made note of address, occupants' names and ages. Ages of children were recorded accurately whereas those of adults were given to the nearest five-year interval below their actual age. There is usually also an indication of whether the occupant was born in the same area (a simple 'y' or 'n') but no further information.

From 1851, the occupation of residents, marital status, birth place and relationship to the head of house was recorded. In Wales, there was also a question regarding the understanding and use of language recording the use of Welsh, English or both.

The 1911 Census also recorded the number of years a couple had been married and how many live births there had been. This number was then split between those children still living and those deceased. It is likely that as subsequent censuses become available for viewing (each revealed after 100 years) further information will be visible subsequent to the devising of additional questions.

Most names are easy to trace using an on-line search engine but it has to be remembered that the early census returns were completed by an enumerator who went from door to door gathering the required information. Many occupants did not read or write so verification of the spelling of names was impossible and simple phonetics determined the names recorded. First names were sometimes the 'shortened' names given by the family; Lucy for Louise, Betty for Elizabeth. With this possible confusion coupled with mis-transcriptions (where, understandably, errors have been made by transcribers entering numerous names and other data for on-line searches) finding ancestors can sometimes be harder than might be imagined – in my experience, persistence usually pays off.

The 1939 Survey

War was declared in September 1939 and as a direct result of this, a register was taken that listed the personal details of every civilian in Great Britain. It was an important tool in coordinating the war effort at home. The enumerators issued identity cards as they collected the information, which was also used to organise rationing. The information gathered has now been transcribed and is searchable via subscription (discussed in Chapter 6). Although most can now be seen, not all residents can be viewed. Details given include date of birth (day/month/year), occupation (sometimes even their place of work) and address.

For women all other surnames are given (maiden name/previous married names).

At some point in history the register has also been amended and written above some women's names in coloured pen are all subsequent surnames. As with the Census, it is possible to see neighbouring households.

Parish records

Most parish records can be found at the relevant local record office. As with other records, some were lost during wartime bombing. Many have now been transcribed and photographed and can be viewed on-line (see Chapter 6) saving a great deal of research time.

The parish records vary in the amount of information given. Baptisms, marriages and burials were entered into a parish book, usually located at the church.

Early baptism entries often only gave the date, father's full name and child's first name.

Later, the mother's first name was given. This was the Baptism of twin sons in 1792, unusually for this time, the father's occupation is also provided:

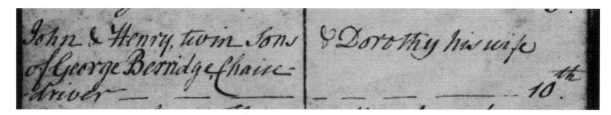

By 1908, as illustrated below, the family's address was also included in the parish entry.

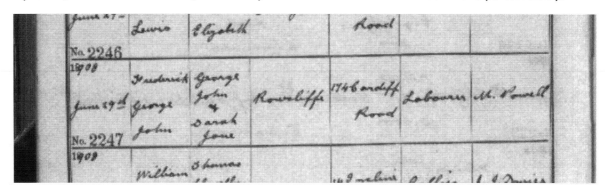

It must be remembered that although an infant was usually baptised in the weeks soon after birth, there was sometimes a considerable time delay when a number of siblings were baptised at the same time, so the date of baptism does not always accurately determine the date of birth.

There are frequently two entries for a marriage: to record the reading of the Banns and the actual marriage ceremony. Again, the amount of information recorded can vary considerably from just the two names and date to the addition of age, occupation, whether previously married (widow or widower) or requiring parental permission due to young age. The entry will also disclose whether those marrying could sign their names.

In the following example from 1790, it is recorded that the couple indicated their consent by 'mark' rather than signature:

Similarly, in 1813, the couple below signed with a 'mark'. In this case they are described as widower and widow.

Finally, the couple detailed below, in 1815, required the consent of their parents. Again, they signed with a 'mark'.

In my experience, burials give the least information: usually, just name and date.

Other Church Records

As well as Church of England, many of our ancestors were Non-conformists: Methodist, Strict Baptist or Calvinist. Records were still kept by the respective churches and are now housed at local record offices. For some groups, as baptisms did not take place for infants, it was their births that were generally recorded. I was fortunate that some of these records are so detailed they give not only the names of the parents but also the grandparents. Again, most have been transcribed and more are becoming available as time goes on.

Below is the birth record for John Cooper, born in 1815. The record lists his parents; James and Priscilla Cooper and his mother Priscilla's parents Isaac and Ann Clark. John Growse, a surgeon, and Ann Crooks were present at his birth. James and Priscilla were Strict Baptists living in Ringshall, Suffolk.

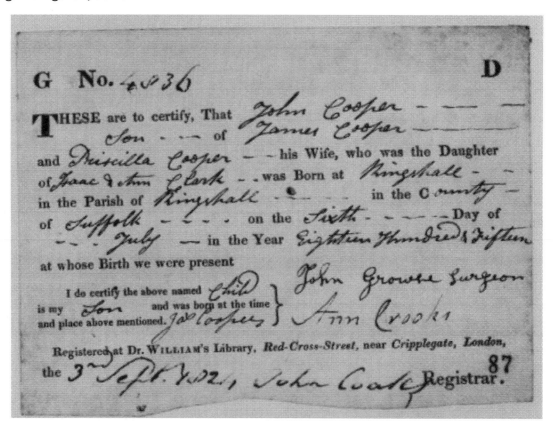

Voters' lists

Voters' lists record those in an area legally able to vote. The earliest voters' lists only include the 'landed' gentry. Home owners were then added and subsequently all men. It was not until 1918 that women of status were added (women had to be over the age of 30 and either house-owners themselves or married to house-owning men) and then finally all over the age of 21 (now 18).

These lists can be of use in placing ancestors but I found little other information forthcoming.

Trade Directories

Directories have been produced by a number of publishers, perhaps the most well-known and accessible are White's, Pigot's and Kelly's Directories.

First published in the early 1800s, the earliest directories covered larger towns and cities. They were produced to give information about the particular locations to visitors. Each location started with a general description of the area and then provided information about churches, schools, transport, shops and other businesses, often giving the names of businessmen and shop-keepers.

Gradually more information was included, with some giving the names of local private residents, particularly the more prominent or wealthier residents.

Directories can be useful in locating ancestors at times between the Censuses or earlier than 1841 when the first available Census was taken. Perhaps most interesting however, is the description of the place in a historical context. This can be invaluable in helping to paint a picture of what it might have been like for ancestors living in a particular location at a specific time.

Transcriptions are available on-line (see Chapter 6) but copies are available for their particular location at local libraries and record offices.

Ships' Passenger Lists

If ancestors emigrated, there are now a large number of ships' passenger lists available for the major shipping routes. These are searchable on some websites (Chapter 6). The records generally give the name of the passenger and other family members travelling with them as well as their age, occupation and destination. It is possible to see when they left their home country and when they arrived at their destination. The name of the ship and senior crew members is also given.

The Research of Others

Many family historians are now putting their information online in one form or another and it is well worth searching for ancestors' names and locations or names and dates. You may also be lucky to find some distant cousins! Some of the subscription sites also link to the family research of others.

One word of advice – if you find something interesting, make a copy and save it. The World Wide Web is continually changing with sites being taken down and put up all the time. If using Windows10, a simple 'screen-shot' can be taken using the 'Snipping Tool' and selecting the part of the screen you want to save by 'dragging' from the top left corner and across to bottom right.

Local Record Offices also house books written by others and these books may include information that you are seeking. I found a research project written by an undergraduate at the nearby university giving me insight into housing and employment in the 1850s for the town where my ancestors lived – so helpful. Those who have already created their family history book often choose to donate a copy to the relevant Record Office – if you are lucky, your family may just be related to theirs.

Other members of your family have already been mentioned as a valuable source of information but you may just find that someone in the family has already done some of the work for you. I was probably more fortunate than most; my mother's cousin Sylvia was a very keen family historian who had written down some of her memories and sent her work to me along with copies of some of her treasured photographs. As a child she had lost her own mother and was raised by her grandparents (my Great Grandparents). Before the days of television and other distractions, she had been immersed in tales of the antics of past generations recounted with passion by her beloved Grandma Ada and Grandpa Arthur. In my own book, when describing some shared ancestors, I was able to include her words verbatim, as quotes. It felt good to ensure that Sylvia's work was not lost and our shared ancestors were recorded in as much detail as possible.

An example of Sylvia's invaluable contribution to my own book:

'George's four daughters all married. The eldest, Rosa, was an elegant, proud girl who became engaged to an attractive young man called Nathaniel Redding, a skilled carver by trade. She committed the unforgiveable sin for a girl in a Victorian Nonconformist family of becoming pregnant before the wedding. The shame of this was too much for her, and shortly after they were married the young couple emigrated to Australia, where Nathaniel had been promised a good job through an advertisement. On arrival, however, he found that there was no job. His correspondent, having been deceived himself over promised work, had decided to play the same trick on someone else. As a result, their early days were a great struggle; Nathaniel was forced to work on the roads as a labourer, but in time they made good, and had a family of one son and several daughters. The son, also Nathaniel, was killed in the first War. He was said to have enlisted in the Anzac Brigade because he was fascinated by the photograph of one of his English cousins, Lily Singleton, and hoped for an opportunity to meet her. They did indeed meet, when he was on leave, and even got engaged, but he was killed soon afterwards and contact with his family was lost.

Another sister, Daisy, married a very short man named Frederick Eggleton. As she was rather tall, she always walked with a stoop to minimise the difference in height. She and her family emigrated to Australia after the first War, when her eldest daughter Winnie, a pretty, affected and very flirtatious girl, married an Australian soldier, Frank Westbrook.'

Frank Westbrook wrote a small book of poems called 'Anzac and After' of which we have a copy. In it, Frank wrote about Australia and his war-time experiences. Despite taking part at Gallipoli and losing many friends, it appears that his attitude to the war remained unquestioning.' [Sylvia]

Older relatives will have so much knowledge about their own elders. It is a source of information that is such a loss if not sought.

Useful Websites

There are a great many websites available for those trying to research their family history. In this chapter I will describe those that I found the most useful.

Familysearch (https://www.familysearch.org)

This is the website developed and maintained by the Church of the Latter-day Saints, a church which places great importance on knowledge of your ancestral roots. The site is free to search and has an amazing range of information, mainly for the USA and UK but including some records from other regions. This information includes:

Births, Deaths and Marriages – Included are many parish and non-conformist records and all post 1837 certificate names and dates.

Census and Lists – All UK Census records have now been transcribed. I believe that the same is true for the USA but did not personally need to search these. From my experience, the transcriptions are predominantly accurate and easy to search. It is possible to see all occupants living at an address along with their age and occupation. It is not possible to view the actual enumerator's entry (or head of house submission for 1911).

Migration and Naturalisation – Many passenger lists are included, the vast majority for the USA but also for Canada, Australia, Belgium and other countries. USA state naturalisation records are also searchable.

Military – World War 1 and World War 2 records for the UK and USA as well as the US Civil War and Mexican War can be searched. Unfortunately, some UK World War 1 records were lost in World War 2 bombings.

Other – A variety of other records are available such as electors lists and some probate records and these are being added to each month.

Find My Past (https://www.findmypast.co.uk)

This is a subscription site but usually offers a short free trial period if you want to try before you buy. The subscriptions vary in price according to which record collections you want to have access to. I was lucky that the majority of the family were to be found in the UK so I didn't really need to access the 'worldwide' records. There are also varying amounts of time that you can sign up for - the shorter the time period the more the monthly fee. Personally, I signed up for one month at a time. As a newly retired person, I could dedicate many hours to my research and so made very good use of the site during the period it was available to me. I did find the access to 1939 records useful so decided that the package best for me would include this.

Find My Past's records are vast and I found them to be well transcribed making them easy to search. The most amazing aspect is that many records have been photographed so it is possible to see the actual document (sometimes including the actual signature of an ancestor!). I found the site easy to navigate and it was really important to my personal research.

The site has the option of adding your own tree and will make links and suggestions for relevant records to view. I did this for one small part of my tree that was causing difficulty but was a little reluctant to make the site the main store for the whole tree, feeling that it may lock me in to feeling that I should remain a subscribing member for life! It's obviously a personal thing and others may be very happy with this aspect of the site.

The site covers most records mentioned under 'Familysearch' but includes many photos of these records. It is surprising how much more can be gleaned from the original. In addition, the site also has records for:

Legal and Courts

Electoral Rolls

Land and Estate Taxes

Rate Books

Surveys

Directories and Almanacs

Newspapers and Magazines

Education and Work – Apprenticeships, Trade Associations, Schools

Institutions – Schools, Workhouses, Prison Registers

Military – Enlistment papers, Medals

Ancestry (https://www.ancestry.com)

This is another great site for the vast range of information and links to others who may be researching the same ancestors. I found that, locally, our library had subscribed to the site and members had free access. It was a little restricting because the library (or perhaps it was rules set in the library's subscription) set a one-hour limit per member each day. I used it for searching the difficult to find ancestors, so went in with a definite 'to do' list which made good use of the time available. I believe that some of the larger record offices have unrestricted access to the site.

Similar to 'Find My Past', Ancestry has a range of subscription periods for different ranges of record collections. It may also be possible to try a short subscription-free period.

The Genealogist (https://www.thegenealogist.co.uk)

The Genealogist has many records but the ones I found particularly valuable were the UK Tithe maps and associated records.

Unfortunately, my personal searches for Census records on this site were particularly frustrated by poor transcribing. On many occasions, I had located the family record using 'Familysearch.com' and just wanted to see the actual photographic record. I knew all the names and their occupations as well as the address but mis-spelling led to great difficulty finding the record. It seemed as if transcription had been achieved electronically, so poor handwriting was not recognised from knowledge of the language (Smith transcribed as Snuith and 'Gardener retired' as 'Garderness Rebering'). There were also sequencing issues with names being ascribed to the wrong people:

Marion Frankland followed by George Knights, was transcribed, Marion Knights followed by George Loades.
So, finding George Knights, the retired gardener, was rather problematic!

The Newspaper Archive (https://www.britishnewspaperarchive.co.uk/)

This is a fascinating resource for finding historic facts about the lives of UK ancestors. Just like today, not everyone finds their name in the newspapers but I was amazed at what I was able to find:

The wedding of Margaret Morris and John Rees in Aberdare, Wales 1908

A very pretty and interesting wedding was solemnized on Sunday morning last at Carmel English Baptist Chapel, Aberdare, the happy pair being Mr. John D. Rees, electrician at The Marquis of Bute Collieries, Aberdare, and Miss Margaret (Maggie) Morris, eldest daughter of Mr. and Mrs. Arthur Morris, 17, Duke-street. The marriage was celebrated by the Rev. A. B. Kinsey, B.A., in the presence of Mr. Geo. G. Jones, Registrar, and the wedding was attended by a goodly number of Mr. and Mrs. Rees' friends. The bride, who was given away by her father, was charmingly attired in a travelling costume of navy-blue cloth and blue glace silk hat (trimmed with roses) to match. Mr. William Jenkins (Abernant), brother-in-law of the bridegroom, acted as best man; and the bride was attended by her bridesmaids, Miss Maude Morris, of Oxford (sister): Miss Flossie Morris, Llanelly, sister; Miss Dolly Morris, sister; Miss Emily Singleton (cousin), Miss Gertrude Davies, R.A.M., Llanelly (cousin), and Miss Minnie Edwards, also of Llanelly (cousin). Amongst others present were: Mrs. Agnes Smith, Llanelly (aunt of the bride), Messrs. David James Morris and Trevor Morris (brothers), Mrs. Jenkins (sister of the bridegroom), Miss Jennie Rees, of the Railway Bar Hotel; Miss D. Bryce, Compton House; Mr. Gwilym Mandry, Ystradgynlais; Mr. Fred Davies, Aberaman, and Mr. James Crowley, Aberdare. The whole of the party were afterwards entertained to a sumptuous breakfast at the home of the bride's parents, where all joined in best wishes for the happiness and prosperity of the happy pair. The wedding presents received by both bride and bridegroom were numerous and costly. The honeymoon is being spent at the Mumbles and elsewhere in West Wales. We extend to Mr. and Mrs. Rees our sincere congratulations.

Aberdare Leader, 1908

Thomas Kinnersley's wager in a public house in Shropshire

'Amateur Reaping – A correspondent sends us the following:-

"On the 22nd Aug., being Ludlow fair-day, a party of gentlemen met at the Elephant and Castle Commercial Inn to regale themselves. During the evening the conversation was chiefly on the harvest, and finally on the propriety of mowing wheat – a practice resorted to in the greatest part of that neighbourhood. Mr T. Kinnersley of Clunton, son of the late T. Kinnersley, Esq. of Preston Wynne, near Hereford, remarked the inutility of mowing wheat when men were to be found that could cut with the broad hook an acre per day, which gave rise to the question, "Who can?" Mr Kinnersley replied, "I can." Some of the party being incredulous as to the feat being performed, a wager was laid between Mr Kinnersley and Mr Tait of the Bach, which amounted to a considerable sum. Mr Kinnersley was backed by E. Downes, Esq., Brooms; W. Blockley, Esq., Broadstone; R. Carter, Esq., Ashford, &c. On Mr Tait's side were John Bishop, Esq., Sibdon Castle; Mr M. Evans, landlord of the inn, &c. The feat was to be performed on the Wednesday following. Mr T. Langslow of Abcott-hall, who was present, with his wonted good nature kindly gave permission for an acre of wheat in his field to become the scene of action. Mr K. was allowed from five o'clock a.m. until eight o'clock p.m. E. Dawes, Esq., New-house, who measured the ground, was chosen as referee, and A. Woolley, Esq., Abcott, umpire. The wheat stood well, though a strong crop. The amateur reaper, undaunted, entered the field, and, as the village clock struck five, he commenced his laborious undertaking, and nobly won his wager in 13$\frac{1}{2}$ hours, being an hour and a half under the limited time, apparently without fatigue, and was loudly cheered by his friends and supporters.'

-Salopian Journal, September 1842-

Arthur Morris's notice of bankruptcy 1900

'Gazette News
BANKRUPTCY ACTS 1883 and 1890 – RECEIVING ORDERS
Arthur Morris, 17, Duke Street, Aberdare, plumber, tin and zinc ware manufacturer.
Henry Pitt, 118, Portmanmoor Road, Cardiff, car-driver, formerly licenced victualler.
Joseph Griffiths …'

Aberdare Leader

…and the subsequent notification of the granting of a patent for his invention 1907

Patent No. 8,028

April 23rd, 1894 - A. Morris, Aberdare, Glamorganshire   Oil lamps and Match-holders

This relates to those miners' lamps which are provided with a removable shank by which the lamp is held, and comprises the combination of a match receptacle with the lamp. A shank is made in two separate parts, one forming the match receptacle, and is screw-threaded to correspond either with a reservoir mount or with a burner mount. The shank may be made in one piece, closed at the end by a removable stopper.

Aberdare Leader

A hearing prior to deportation from Ipswich, Suffolk, to Australia 1845

> 'Thomas Neech & Andrew Turner of Willingham were indicted on the 29ᵗʰ June at Beccles for stealing two sheep the property of Mr Gibson of Willingham. It appears that they were ewes. Acquitted but remanded to the Ipswich Sessions.'

The website is accessed through subscription and again cost varies according to the period secured. This is probably best done once your other research has been completed. You'll then have a better knowledge of where your ancestors were living and the likely events happening. All this information will help you with search terms. Personally, I found that being prepared and dedicating time to the searches meant that a shorter subscription period was necessary.

Commonwealth War Graves Association (https://www.cwgc.org)

If you have UK ancestors who were lost in wartime it is most likely that you will find them listed on the Commonwealth War Graves Association website. The site lists the known information about where and when they lost their lives, where they are buried or the war memorial that includes their names. Sometimes there is a photograph of the war memorial. Next of kin and their address is also sometimes available.

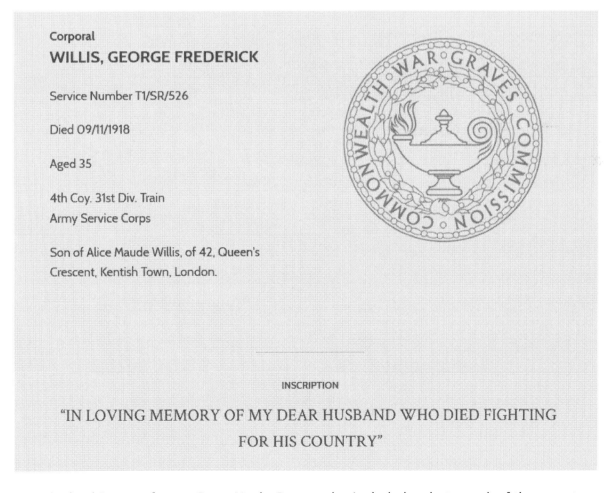

Corporal
WILLIS, GEORGE FREDERICK

Service Number T1/SR/526

Died 09/11/1918

Aged 35

4th Coy. 31st Div. Train
Army Service Corps

Son of Alice Maude Willis, of 42, Queen's Crescent, Kentish Town, London.

INSCRIPTION

"IN LOVING MEMORY OF MY DEAR HUSBAND WHO DIED FIGHTING FOR HIS COUNTRY"

Amazingly, this entry for my Great Uncle George also included a photograph of the cemetery and a plan so that I am able to locate his grave on visiting the site.

Other free websites that I found useful were:

The National Archives (http://www.nationalarchives.gov.uk)

The National Archives hold a wealth of UK information from service records to wills, court cases and work records. Some are available to view in full, others give just brief details of the record held for identification purposes.

It is possible to request copies of archived records. A set fee is payable for a preliminary request (payable whether or not you go ahead with the purchase of copies). This is followed by a quote for the requested records to be copied and sent to you. Smaller items can easily be copied and the cost can be worth the additional information revealed. Beware however, that some of the archived records (court cases in particular) can be many pages long and written on parchment pages that measure almost a metre square. A record that I sought held a copying price of over £350! I was somewhat aggrieved at having paid the preliminary fee as that was money lost, but made the journey to Kew, in London, to see the record for myself. I have to say, if you are able to make the trip, handling the original document is an experience in itself. The environment is well lit, with plenty of space to lay out the antique records and admire the meticulously executed copperplate script. For a small fee, you are able to photograph documents yourself.

This is a hand-written court case transcript, 1845. Viewed at the National Archives, in Kew, London.

If you do plan to visit the National Archives, make sure you read the latest advice on the website regarding opening times, booking records ahead of your visit (some are held offsite) and that you have the correct ID to obtain a card for access to the archive rooms.

GenUKi (https://www.genuki.org.uk)

This is a free reference site with a huge amount of information, advice regarding access to further records and other valuable genealogical material.

Cindis List (https://www.cyndislist.com)

Another free site, Cindis List has a role as genealogical gateway. It has a great deal of information about and links to hundreds of useful genealogical websites.

FreeUKGenealogy (https://www.freeukgenealogy.org.uk/) :

FreeCEN, FreeBMD and FreeReg

Again, this is a tremendous resource and increasingly holds freely available and searchable Census records (FreeCen), Birth, Death and Marriage records - post 1937 (FreeBMD) and Parish records before this date (FreeReg). The records have grown rapidly over the years and it has become one of the leading free UK genealogy sites.

Rootsweb (https://home.rootsweb.com)

A free site that is particularly good for contacting others and seeking information through its 'message boards'.

Find A Grave (https://www.findagrave.com)

This is a worldwide resource with details of all the legible graves in locations that have been covered so far. It is extensive but still limited as the area to be covered is so vast. If you are lucky, you will be able to find the memorial or photographed gravestone of an ancestor.

Gravestone Photos (https://www.gravestonephotos.com)

For my own UK research, I found this was the most useful website. The site is still limited to the cemeteries that have been photographed by volunteers but is growing rapidly and if lucky, the information is really helpful. To check whether the cemetery you are looking for has been recorded, the site is searchable by country, state, county, city, town or village.

Volunteers list all the grave monuments within a cemetery (legible when they were photographed). It is possible to see all the names on a grave monument and their relationships to each other.

The headstone photograph can be viewed on the website but it is also possible to request a high-quality photograph for your records.

Family Tree Software Tools

GenoPro (https://www.genopro.com/)

There are many packages that can be used to create your family tree. I tried two. The first (shown later) although attractive, would not have been suitable for using in a book. I decided on GenoPro, with a once only purchase price and online support, it gave what I was looking for.

The tree produced is in the traditional tree shape:

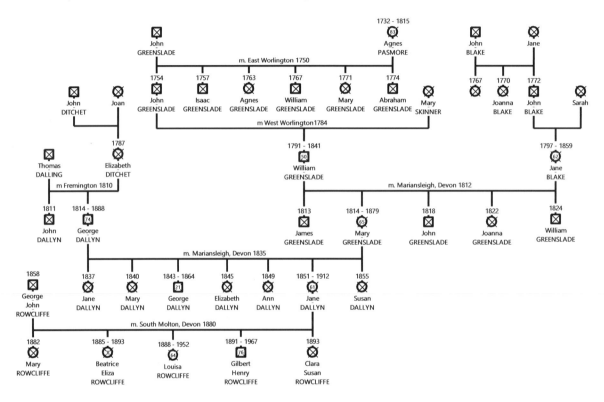

It has the option of displaying occupations:

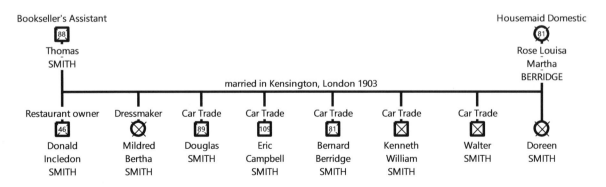

25

there is also the option of displaying photos:

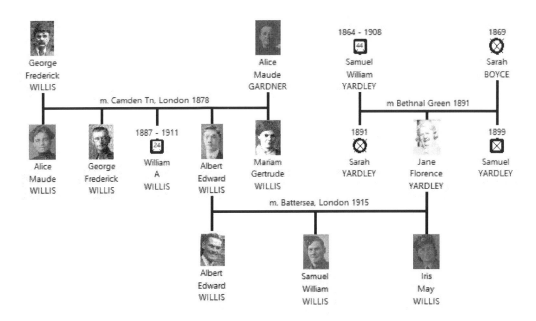

This computer program can be downloaded from the GenoPro website. My own first download was free of charge but I upgraded to the latest package that included the photograph capability. Compared with some other tools it was, at the time, low cost and represented good value for money. Using the program, each person on the tree can be 'clicked on' to reveal all related details. This allows the program to be a main source of all your information. However, for the purposes of making a family history book, I'll limit my comments here to those of most use on a two-dimensional basis.

GenoPro is designed for use by family historians and also those interested in family dynamics such as social workers and health professionals. Due to this there are menus that allow the highlighting of those with particular illnesses. These are colour-coded. Although the investigation of hereditary medical conditions may not be in your remit, the colour coding includes pink and blue – ideal for indicating the sex of each family member. I found this invaluable when printing my family tree wall chart and included a copy of the jpg image on my disc (see Chapter 11).

For display purposes, it is easiest to focus on your own ancestral line. In this way, siblings are included but not their wives, husbands or children. This makes the tree easier to follow and reduces the size significantly. There may be sections of your tree that you wish to add additional detail to. It can be done by creating a new tree for the group of focus in your discussion. 'Highlighting' an area of your original tree and 'copying' into a new tree page will give the bare bones of the new family group for you to add to. Each chapter of your book can begin in this way, showing just the family group for the chapter in hand. The tree can be entered into your book as a 'screen-shot' JPG image or if 'highlighted' and 'copied' can be 'pasted' onto your page.

GedHtree

This was another downloadable resource, unfortunately no longer available but it gives an idea of other tree presentations that have been developed. This particular resource was intended for the creation of a family history web page and was suitable for recording all genealogical information. The tree produced by this program is attractive but restricted in terms of book production as allows only four generations to be viewed at one time in a horizontal progression from left to right.

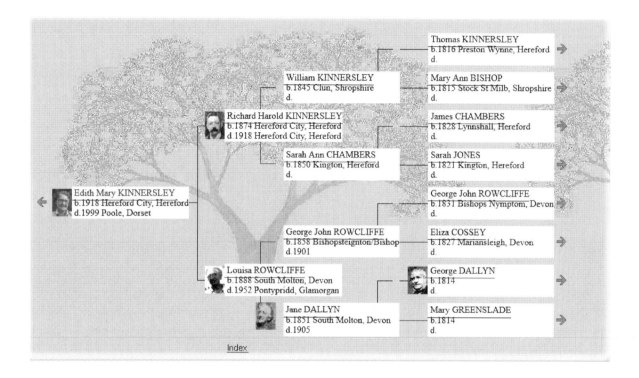

There are many more formats available. Just check that the display is as you intend and it is flexible enough to deal with those more complex families!

Visiting Ancestral Villages and Finding Graves

Once the names of your ancestors have been found and you have gathered together information from a range of sources, a visit to the locations is invaluable. It can be the source of many photographs that will bring your ancestral story to life. I also found it quite amazing to feel that I was walking in the footsteps of relatives. I could imagine the wedding as I stood in the village church and in some cases see the actual houses they lived in.

Before visiting an area, it is advisable to print a copy of a local map and annotate it showing the important addresses. This could include homes, churches, cemeteries, workplaces or schools that you know played a part in your ancestors' lives. If there are neighbouring villages that need visiting or perhaps a local library, museum or record office, make an itinerary so that your time is well spent.

There will be many locations across the different ancestral lines and it is at this point that I think it best to focus on one at a time. This way names and dates will be easier to remember and you will find that you don't constantly need to be looking back at your records. A printout of the part of the family tree being focused on is also vital as it can easily be carried with you and used to jot down things of interest relating to individuals.

A digital camera or mobile phone that is capable of taking good digital images is essential. When making your book, it is these images that will captivate your readers and help them to experience the things that you are able to in person.

As an example, my own family research took me to Hereford where generations of the Kinnersley and Chambers families had lived. The story came to life with the addition of photos taken and time spent at the Hereford Record Office:

Thomas Kinnersley worked a farm at Eaton Bishop just outside the town of Hereford. The farm is still maintained and this photograph was taken from the road as we walked past, admiring the beauty of the area.

Farm at Eaton Bishop, as it is today.

After losing his farm and income, Thomas Kinnersley's family found refuge at The Conningsby Almshouses. The Almshouses still exist and part of the building has been turned into a museum. The tiny dwellings have also been combined to make them large enough for comfortable modern living. The chapel and courtyard with original water tap were open to view and the small museum shed light on the history of its link to the Conningsby Hospital.

Conningsby Almshouses and chapel, Hereford

Thomas was able to start trading as a butcher and eventually left the Almshouses to set up his own shop. The shop has now been altered to make flats but the outside still shows the old shop window.

The Butcher's shop still exists but has been converted into flats.

The grave of Thomas and his wife Mary Ann was found at Hereford Cemetery. Staff at the Cemetery Office had helped us to locate the grave on a plan but finding it proved more problematic than expected. The grave was hidden under the edge of a large bush and covered with ivy and brambles. I wished that I had taken gloves and secateurs! In the end we managed to clear the vegetation and were touched by the words on the headstone.

In Loving Memory of

MARY ANN

The beloved wife of THOMAS KINNERSLEY

Butcher of this city

Who departed this life Sept. 21st 1883

Aged 68 Years

Released at length from cares and lingering pains

Here peaceful sleep a mother's loved remains,

She lived in Jesus and in peace she died.

Her husband's joy, her children's friend and guide.

Thomas's son William married Sarah Chambers at St James Chapel, in Hereford.

St James Chapel, Hereford

They set up home in a terrace in the area. At the time the house was divided into an upstairs and downstairs flat. Thomas and his wife Sarah lived in one part, while Sarah's mother was in another. Sarah's mother (another Sarah) was probably already suffering the effects of Cholera (as detailed on her death certificate) from previous insanitary living conditions.

Thomas and Sarah's home in Hereford, as it is today.

Sarah's mother's grave was found in Hereford Cemetery.

William and Sarah later moved to Eign Farm, where they lived and worked. The farm is no longer in existence but the Hereford Record Office held a historic map showing its position.

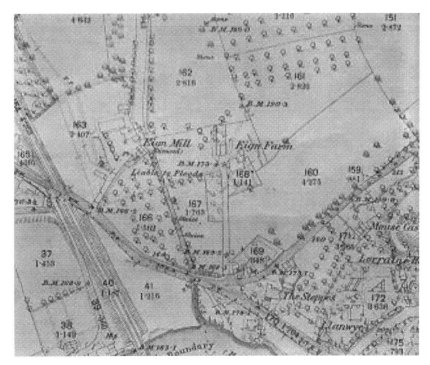

It was Sarah's father, James Chambers who spent many years in the 'Burghill Lunatic Asylum'. It was possible to visit the site of the Asylum. Some of the original buildings have now been made part of a stylish housing development. They have been joined by other houses that incorporate similar patterned brickwork and some of the open space has been preserved.

One of the original Burghill Lunatic Asylum buildings, now modernised.

The records of James' residence at the Asylum giving details of his day to day life and troubles were, amazingly, viewable at the Hereford Record Office.

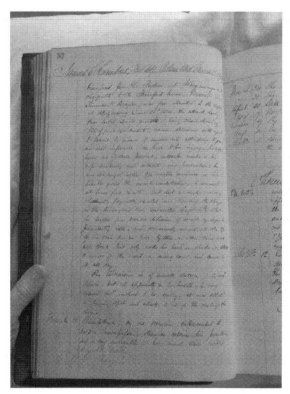

Although the text was not very clear, with time and concentration it could be deciphered and its contents were invaluable in shedding light onto the struggles of this family line.

There may well be locations that are too distant to visit but those within your reach will enrich your story. Following your visit, you will be able to describe places and include images that would not otherwise be available to you. Local record offices may also have information that you were unaware of, such as the Asylum records seen here.

Cemeteries and Churchyards

Some of the previous photos are of headstones that I was able to include in my own family history book.

The location of ancestral graves can sometimes be gleaned from parish and town cemetery records. However, even with accurate names and dates, it is not always possible to know ahead of your visit where an ancestor's grave is. In these cases, looking in the local church graveyard and walking the lines of graves is sometimes the only solution (and can take many patient hours!). If you plan to do this, bear in mind that not all churchyards are beautifully manicured and brambles, tall grass and uneven ground may be what you find. Wellies and stout gardening gloves are a really good idea.

Contacting the town cemetery record office is definitely worth doing. There may be a small charge for staff time taken to look up your ancestor's details but knowing the rough vicinity of the grave location is a real help.

Be aware that even if the location is known, many of the headstones have become illegible. A churchyard we visited in Ringwood, Hants was filled with mostly flat headstones, where the surface of the local stone had been totally eroded.

The headstone marking the grave of Priscilla Cooper (nee Frankland) at Beccles Cemetery. This was found in a wooded part of the cemetery after much searching.

I was very lucky with the headstone of Priscilla Cooper (nee Frankland), in Beccles, Suffolk. The main details were still visible but it probably won't be very long before more of the surface stone is lost.

Local Record Offices

The local record office is always worth visiting. Before the days of comprehensive searchable websites, many hours could be spent looking through meters of microfilm or wading through filing cabinets full of microfiche for Census and Parish records. All these are still available but so much more is held besides.

Old maps, land-ownership records, electoral lists, employment and apprenticeship records – the list goes on. Some record offices have amazing online catalogues that can be searched before you visit, others are not quite so well organised. From my personal experience, they are all run by incredibly helpful staff – you only have to ask.

Old photographs of the local area and books compiled by other genealogists can also be extremely helpful.

Before you visit, it is essential to check opening hours. Many Record Offices are closed on certain days of the week and they may have restricted opening times on the days that they are available.

You will be asked to complete some registration details and will need to provide personal identification (a driver's licence is usually sufficient). A card will then be issued to you for access to the records library. A small fee is often charged if you intend to take photographs of the records you find. As many of the records are irreplaceable, security and care dictate that bags must be placed in lockers. Take with you a pencil, notepad and camera (if you intend taking photos). Protective gloves and book supports will always be available to preserve the most delicate of records.

Tithe maps, Tenant Farmers and Land Owners

Tithe maps refer to maps of English and Welsh towns and parishes. These maps were prepared after the 'Tithe Commutation Act' became law, in 1836. Following the act, tithes could be paid in cash rather than goods. Tithe maps show land ownership and the names of tenant farmers (occupiers) working the land. The Devon Record Office has made these searchable online and includes the written records (schedules) as well as the old maps showing the specific plots of land (identifiable by allocated numbers).

Some websites give access to Tithe maps and local record offices will hold copies for viewing (these are often enormous and need a great deal of space to lay out).

If an ancestor owned or leased land for farming it is these records that will place and identify the size of their land.

In the case of my own ancestor, Mary Pincombe Thorne, her land ownership was for a time in some dispute. The illegitimate heiress of her father's land, she had to undergo court proceedings to establish legal ownership. Her uncles had felt that they were the 'heirs at law'. Finally, after a court hearing in Westminster, Mary's father's Will was upheld.

The schedule shows clearly that at the time the schedule was drawn up, Mary was the legal land-owner. The land was being farmed by tenant farmer Thomas Handcock:

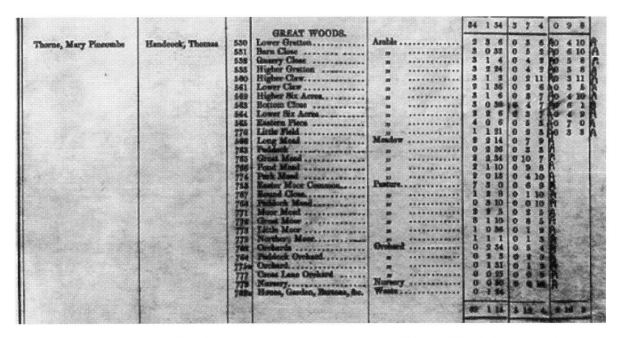

At the time, Mary Pincombe Thorne is shown as the owner of 'Great Woods' an area that includes 29 fields or meadows. Each has an identification number so that it can be found on the associated map. The fifth column shows what was being farmed by the tenant farmer.

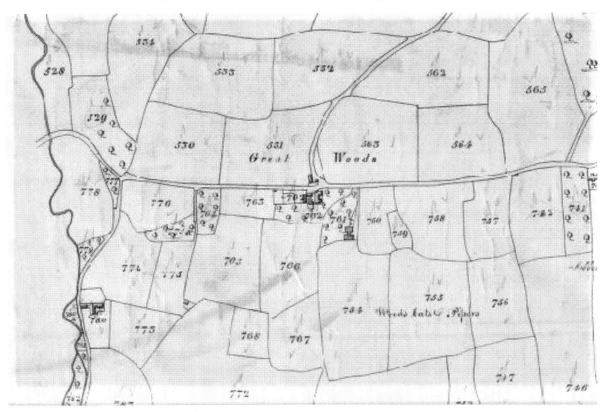

The numbers on the associated map above relate to the fields named in the schedule (so 772 at the very bottom of the map is 'Great Moor' and it is pasture land).

Timelines and the Historical Context

For those reading your family history book, it can be difficult to link the date ancestors lived with what was going on historically at the same time. For this reason, the inclusion of a brief timeline setting out the main historical events is a good idea. The information itself is of course not copyright but lists compiled by others in a particular format should be avoided. To save time, I have included the list I compiled (drawn from a number of sources). If you find it helpful, I am happy for you to use this without seeking permission, in its entirety or with your own additions/deletions.

Historical Timeline

— **1531** Henry VIII head of the newly created Church of England

— **1536** Dissolution of the Monasteries

— **1538** Parish registers kept

— **1588** Spanish Armada destroyed

— **1603** King James VI of Scotland crowned James I of England

— **1605** Gunpowder Plot

— **1620** The Mayflower sailed to the New World

— **1642-1660** Civil War in England

— **1649** Charles I executed - Oliver Cromwell Lord Protector of England

— **1660** Charles II restored as monarch

— **1665-1666** Great Plague followed by Great Fire of London

— **1685** Increase in the migration of Huguenot refugees from France to England.

— **1688-89** William of Orange from Holland crowned King of England

— **1707** England and Wales united with Scotland (United Kingdom)

— **1702** William III succeeded by Anne

— **1714** George I crowned king

— **1752** Gregorian calendar -Year start changed from 25 March to 1 January

— **1754** Lord Hardwicke's Act outlawed marriage outside the Church of England

(except for Quakers and Jews)

— **1756-1762** The Seven Years War in North America

— **1756-1765** Industrial revolution began - invention of the steam engine and the

spinning jenny.

— **1775-1783** American War of Independence

— **1800** Ireland became part of the United Kingdom

— **1805** Battle of Trafalgar

— **1815** Battle of Waterloo (end of Napoleonic Wars)

— **1830** First railways in England

— **1834** Workhouses were established

— **1837** Civil registration of births, marriages, and deaths began

— **1837-1901** Queen Victoria reigned

— **1841** First genealogically useful census

— **1854-1856** Crimean war

— **1863** First underground train in London

— **1877-1902** Boer Wars

— **1914–1918** World War I

— **1939–1945** World War II.

Some historical information might have had a direct impact on your ancestors and is worth investigating to include in your text. In my own book, I was able to find out about the lead up to many people leaving Devon for the US and Canada. There was also the settlement of a large number of Huguenot weavers to the East End of London in their escape from religious persecution. This was the precursor to some of my ancestors working in the silk weaving industry.

It was also interesting to find out that generations marrying in St Pancras Church, in London, actually married in different locations! – the neglected church had been rebuilt due to the gradual, southerly move of the local population, towards Euston Square, away from where the original church had been built. To my surprise, the new church has special recognition by English Heritage for being a significant early example of Greek Revival architecture, greatly influenced by the design of the Acropolis, in Athens!

Use a search engine on the web and you will be surprised what you end up investigating. It will lead to a much more informative and interesting book.

Preparation for Printing

Having put so much time and effort into research and writing your family history book, considerable thought needs to go into your finished creation. If you want the book to be worthy of being passed from generation to generation, so that future members of the family have access to their history, copies need to be well produced and robust.

Layout

'Justifying' the text always gives a more ordered appearance. If you have used Microsoft 'Word' for your writing, 'Justify' can be found under 'Paragraph' ('Home' tab on the menu bar). Using 'Justify' makes the right-hand margin look more uniform.

Text font size is best set at 11 or 12 depending on the chosen font. My choice here is 'Calibri' which I prefer for its clarity. Other good clear fonts include 'Trebuchet', 'Tahoma' and 'Arial'.

Finally, choose your 'Heading' style. It could be the same font but in larger font size and perhaps made bold. In this book and my own family tree book I have chosen Lucinda Handwriting, with the main headings in font size 16.

Once your text is the size you require, photos and text boxes will have been repositioned. The next step is to go through page by page, making changes to image size and spacing to ensure that all page breaks are where you want them and each chapter starts on a new page.

Remember to 'save' regularly – it is a good idea to keep earlier saved versions under separate file names in case changes are made that you later regret.

Additional Pages

The book will need:

- a title page that can include your copyright notice. This should include the copyright symbol, your name and the date. You do not need to register copyright under British law, it is yours by right. A 'rights reserved' sentence is fairly standard - it ensures that your material cannot be used by others without your permission. 'CIP' reference shows that you have complied with the British Library requirements (see Chapter 11). An example can be seen at the beginning of this book.
- a dedication/acknowledgements page if you wish
- a contents page
- a 'foreword' introducing your book
- a 'postscript' or 'afterword' to give a conclusion to your book. I personally prefer 'afterword' as the technical definition of 'postscript' is 'an additional remark at the end of a letter, after the signature and introduced by PS' which implies the addition of something forgotten. However, both seem acceptable in the world of books so the choice is yours.

- You may also wish to include an 'Appendix' of items referred to in your text and an 'Index'.

'Headers and Footers'

With all pages now in place, it is time for the addition of page numbers, usually a 'footer' and located centrally or towards the outer corner on right hand pages (so that flicking through, the numbers are visible). It will be necessary to keep the first couple of pages number free as you will not want a page number on the title page or any initial blank pages. This can be a little tricky but if you follow the 'help' advice with your writing package it is achievable.

Once numbers are on the pages, the contents page can be completed. Alongside each of the chapter names just add the number for its start page.

If you wish, you can now add 'headers' to the pages showing the chapter name. Again, this can be a little tricky as document 'breaks' need to be added before different 'headers' can be added. You may feel that having a 'Contents' page is sufficient for your audience.

Saving Your Book

Check (and get others to check) your book and when completely happy, save the file. This is your finished book and can now be saved as a PDF. In 'Microsoft Word' this is easy to do. When you have the 'save as' screen, locate the 'save as type' drop down box and select 'PDF (*.pdf)'. Not only does this stop the accidental altering of your work but it also reduces the amount of memory it takes, therefore reducing download time (my own 114 A4 pages reduced from 137MB to 8.43MB!). This is the file that can by used to print from.

The Title and Front Cover

The title and design of your front cover are obviously personal taste but must be decided upon. If you have made your focus one particular family then 'The Smith Family History' is a clear front-runner. If, like me, you have researched every part of your own and your partner's family you will have looked in some depth at perhaps 16 plus names. It is then difficult to decide on a name for the title. Perhaps an interesting finding or occurrence could be the inspiration for your book title.

It is definitely good to think of your potential audience. When I started out, I had no intention of making my book available to more than my immediate family and so chose to entitle it 'Apple Pies and Welsh Cakes'. Most family members would be able to identify with the links to particular ancestors (known for their culinary prowess), coupled with the joining of our Welsh and English heritage. It is only now that I have placed books in Record Offices and online that I realise the title doesn't give a great deal of indication as to the content!

My own cover design was a simple A4 creation using Microsoft Word. I was able to import photographs and play with the text style and background colour. This was sufficient for use by the print company I used but needed some format modification for use with Amazon (more details in Chapter 11).

Printing Your Book

A great deal will depend on your budget but don't be disheartened, you don't need to be a millionaire to get your book to the people you want to have it. I'll go through the options I chose myself below although I am sure there are many more that I did not investigate.

Years ago, getting your book into print was difficult and could cost several thousand pounds. The term often used for this 'paid for' book production was 'Vanity Publishing'. Unscrupulous companies, set up explicitly to exploit gullible authors, would (and still do!) offer a 'free' manuscript assessment and (of course) would provide back a glowing appraisal. Often, they would infer that wealth and fame were only a short distance away. All that was required was the cheque.

The following, has nothing to do with 'Vanity Publishing'. You now have a manuscript and you are going to publish it yourself. In fact, you may not actually wish to make it available to the general public but if you do that is fine too. The total cost should be at the most a few hundred pounds and that can be brought down to virtually nothing depending on how to choose to publish your book.

Hard-back Books - self-funded

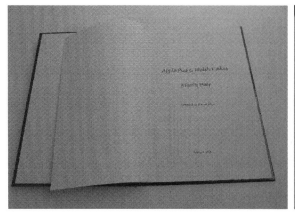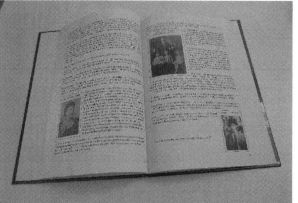

A personal family history book is an item that will be treasured. If you are able, having a hard-back copy printed on good quality paper will give the book longevity, allowing it to be passed between family members and eventually on to subsequent generations. I decided to have fifty copies printed. This was sufficient for immediate family as well as some more distant family members and included all of those who had in any way contributed to my research. There were a few left over, just in case I'd inadvertently forgotten anyone from my list. Don't forget to include yourself!

I searched the internet for online print companies and asked for quotes and samples to be sent to me. Being located in the UK, I made sure that the companies I approached were also UK based. The company I chose was 'Bookprinting.co.uk' but there are many more out there and you might find one that suits your needs better. Many sites have online calculators that allow you to enter the size and number of pages. You are then able to play with quality of paper, cover etc. to see how each affects the cost.

Look for a printing company that includes a physical proof copy (viewing a PDF will just be like looking at what you submitted yourself). To be able to handle the book, feel the weight and quality of pages, look at how the pictures have printed and check for any errors that may have occurred is really important – it is definitely too late to make changes once all the copies are with you!

Check the company's reviews, looking for remarks about quality and staff availability and helpfulness. I have to say; my own experience was positive from start to finish. At the time of writing, a very high quality, hard-back, black and white book with satin paper (producing excellent images) cost about £11.00 a copy.

Please read the section headed 'ISBN Numbers' for details about whether you will need an ISBN number for your book.

Before distributing the books, you may wish to consider adding a CD that has a JPG image of your entire family tree. Those with access to a PC can zoom in to see how the family fits together. You can easily source CDs, self-adhesive labels and paper cases. A quick search online will find you the correct proforma to create your own design for printing your labels (I used the same pictures of ancestors that I had used for the front cover of the book).

You can also consider including a full 'PDF' of your book on the disc. Relatives can then be told that if they are aware of others (perhaps more distant relatives) who would like to read the book, a copy can be forwarded on, attached to an email.

Soft-back Books

Producing your soft-back book can be done using a print company (as described above) and self-funded, but if you want your books to be accessed by relatives living further afield, you don't have the resources to self-fund and would prefer individuals to buy their own copy or you want multiple copies to distribute at lower cost, you may prefer to use an online resource such as that offered by 'Amazon.co.uk.'.

In tandem with having high-quality books produced for direct relatives, I decided that it would be good to make my book accessible to others who might be researching some of the same family groups in similar locations. Using Amazon, it was possible to upload my 'file' and make my book 'Apple Pies and Welsh Cakes' available for purchase.

Some print companies require a minimum purchase (perhaps 50 copies) of the printed book, but with Amazon there is no need to buy any copies at all (although that rather defeats the object of the exercise!). You can also buy a 'proof' copy of the book at print cost. At the time of writing, a typical one hundred-page, black and white book is around £2.00. Not only is the printing cheap but there is no up-front cost either.

ISBN Numbers

If you have chosen to print your book as a hardback or by using a publisher other than Amazon then the first thing you need to do is decide whether the book is going to be for more than just family members. If it is only for family and friends then it does NOT need an ISBN number. In fact, even if you sell the book yourself it still technically does not need an ISBN number. If, however, you intend it to be available for sale through booksellers or you wish to lodge copies with local libraries, then you need to acquire an ISBN number.

Sadly, single ISBN numbers are not cheap. At the time of writing, a single ISBN costs nearly £90, whereas a block of ten is only £60.00 more. ISBN numbers can be purchased online through the 'ISBN Agency UK' at www.nielsenisbnstore.com/home/isbn. If you are planning to publish a hardback and a softback, or maybe have other ideas that you may like to turn into print at a later date, it could be better to buy a block of ten - they never expire.

For elsewhere in the world there is a local national ISBN agency. If you go to the UK agency (above) they have a link to a list of national agencies all over the world. I do not think the rules (or cost) change much between them. You only need to allocate one ISBN to your book to cover world-wide distribution.

A caveat with ISBN numbers is that any change (other than correcting minor errata) entails using a new ISBN number. So, if you publish your book as a paperback and then publish exactly the same book with a hardback cover or as a different size, you need a new ISBN. If you add a new chapter or more pictures, you need a new ISBN. Again, consider this when deciding whether you need to buy a block of ten ISBN numbers.

In the UK, when you publish a book with an ISBN number you must, by law, deposit a copy with the National Library under a scheme called 'Legal Deposit'. In fact, if your book looks interesting enough, then other major libraries can also claim free copies up to a maximum of six in total. While this is a cost to you, it does mean that your work is saved as part of the national book archive and is available for research for the foreseeable future. One ISBN means one deposit. So, if you publish your book as a hardback and a paperback then you will need to make two 'Legal Deposits'.

If you are publishing on Amazon, you always need an ISBN number. But the good news is that they provide an optional free ISBN. The only disadvantage of this is that it locks you into selling through Amazon. If this is not a problem for you then it is obviously the cheapest route. The only 'chicken and egg' issue here is that you need to start creating your book on Amazon to get the ISBN number, which you then need to add to your manuscript before uploading it.

The rear cover - showing the position of the ISBN bar code.

With Amazon you need to set up a KDP account (sign up/in at kdp.amazon.com). Then select 'create a new paperback'. Most fields are self-explanatory. On the second page you get to enter both your PDF manuscript and a cover. You can create a cover on-line immediately using Amazon tools. It is straight forward though somewhat limiting to the given formats. If this is not a problem for you then this is the easiest and quickest way to go.

If you plan building your own cover then the best policy is to download the size template (Amazon auto-produces this for you based on your page count) and then edit this in a program like 'Paint.net' (free to download) or 'Gimp' (free to download) or Photoshop. Getting a good cover is arguably the hardest part of the book creation for those inexperienced in the use of photo-editing so, unless you feel the need to absolutely define your cover yourself, using the in-built cover creator is by far the easiest solution.

When you have entered the manuscript, cover and details of price, markets etc, do NOT immediately publish the book. Instead order a proof. Proofs (as illustrated) come with a 'Not for Resale' band around the centre of the cover. The band is obviously not present in normally purchased copies.

When you get the proof, check it for errors. If there are some, fix them, re-upload the manuscript/cover files and repeat the process.

When you are happy with the proof, click the 'magic' button marked 'Publish'. Your book (barring problems) will be published within 72 hours.

At the time of writing, as the author you can buy up to 500 copies of the book at print price (without the 'Not for Resale' band). For a minimum spend, postage cost is also waved. So, if you plan to give them away to record offices or libraries or meet your legal obligation to deposit them with the National Library this is the cheapest way to go.

The books produced by Amazon are of good quality with laminated card covers and opaque brilliant white paper. They are produced and sent direct to purchasers.

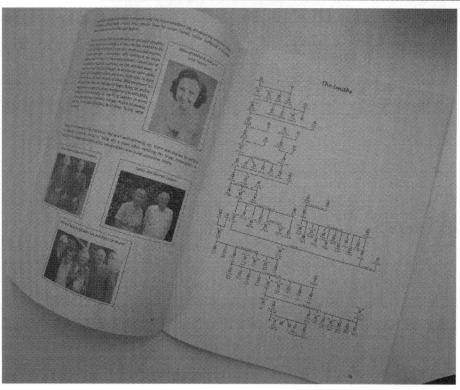

E-books

You may prefer to make your book available as an e-book. Setting up to publish an e-book in Amazon is virtually the same as for printing a physical book with the exception that you do NOT need an ISBN. You can allocate one of your own if you so wish but it is not a necessary requirement. Remember, you CANNOT use the same ISBN for an e-book to that for your physical book.

Publishing e-books that are dominated by text is relatively easy and reliable. However, your manuscript will probably contain a significant number of images. You can upload the 'DOCX' file to create an e-book, but personally, I have never managed to get a good representation of an image-heavy manuscript this way. You can try it and see what you get using the 'Preview' tool but the images can distort the positioning of the text leading to a number of 'hanging' paragraphs. You can reformat your text/images but this is far from simple.

Fortunately, there is a simpler way. You can 'download' an Amazon tool called 'Kindle Create'. This runs on your PC or MAC and processes your 'PDF' into a print replica. There are a couple of caveats here but I will cover them at the end.

After starting 'Kindle Create', select 'New Project from File', then select 'create text books, travel guides, cookbooks, music books'.

Here you simply upload your 'PDF' file. The program creates an e-book version which is an exact replica of your 'PDF'. After you are happy with the presented version click 'Publish' and this then will make you a 'KPF' file from your 'PDF' file. This 'KPF' file is what you need to upload as your manuscript file to Amazon when you create your e-book.

There are some disadvantages:

- Older 'Kindles' may not be able to cope with the 'KPF' file (most 'Kindles' do).

- The presented e-book is a replica of your 'PDF' so the reader cannot change the font size like they can normally. If your 'PDF' is set up for A4 then be careful with the font size. It may be a little too small. It may well be better to re-format your manuscript as A5 just for this process, or increase the font size. Keep this new modified manuscript separate from the one used to publish your physical book.

- Page numbering may have changed. Watch out for discrepancies between page numbers in the e-book and the page numbers given in the chapters index. If you spot errors, amend as required in the e-book-specific manuscript. It may even be best to remove page numbering from your modified e-book-specific manuscript altogether.

Remember you do not have to publish both your e-book and physical book at the same time.

You can upload and modify the manuscript as many times as you like until you are happy with it. Always use the available 'Preview' tools to give you confidence.

Afterword

When your book is finally complete, I hope you experience as much joy as I did in sharing it with your relatives. The feed-back from everyone was amazing and the bonds that bind us together seem to have grown stronger than ever.

It remains for me to share a beautiful text that I found on the internet, for it clearly applies to you the reader, writer of your family's story. It is attributed to author Della M Cummings Wright, 1943:

'We are the chosen. In each family there is one who seems called to find the ancestors – to put flesh on their bones and make them live again, to tell the family story and to feel that somehow they know and approve.

To me, doing genealogy is not a cold gathering of facts but, instead, breathing life into all who have gone before.

We are the story tellers of the tribe. All tribes have one.

We have been called by our genes. Those who have gone before cry out to us: tell our story. So we do. In finding them, we somehow find ourselves. How many graves have I stood before now and cried? I have lost count. How many times have I told the ancestors you have a wonderful family you would be proud of us? How many times have I walked up to a grave and felt somehow there was love there for me?

I cannot say.

It goes beyond just documenting facts. It goes to who am I and why do I do the things I do. It goes to seeing a cemetery about to be lost forever to weeds and indifference and saying I can't let this happen. The bones here are bones of my bone and flesh of my flesh. It goes to doing something about it. It goes to pride in what our ancestors were able to accomplish. How they contributed to what we are today. It goes to respecting their hardships and losses, their never giving in or giving up, their resoluteness to go on and build a life for their family. It goes to deep pride that they fought to make and keep us a Nation.

It goes to a deep and immense understanding that they were doing it for us. That we might be born who we are. That we might remember them. So we do. With love and caring and scribing each fact of their existence, because we are them and they are us. So, as a scribe is called, I tell the story of my family. It is up to that one called in the next generation to answer the call and take their place in the long line of family storytellers.

That is why I do genealogy, and that is what calls those young and old to step up and put flesh on the bones.'

So, it seems that you are destined to write that book! ......

Made in the USA
San Bernardino, CA
07 May 2019